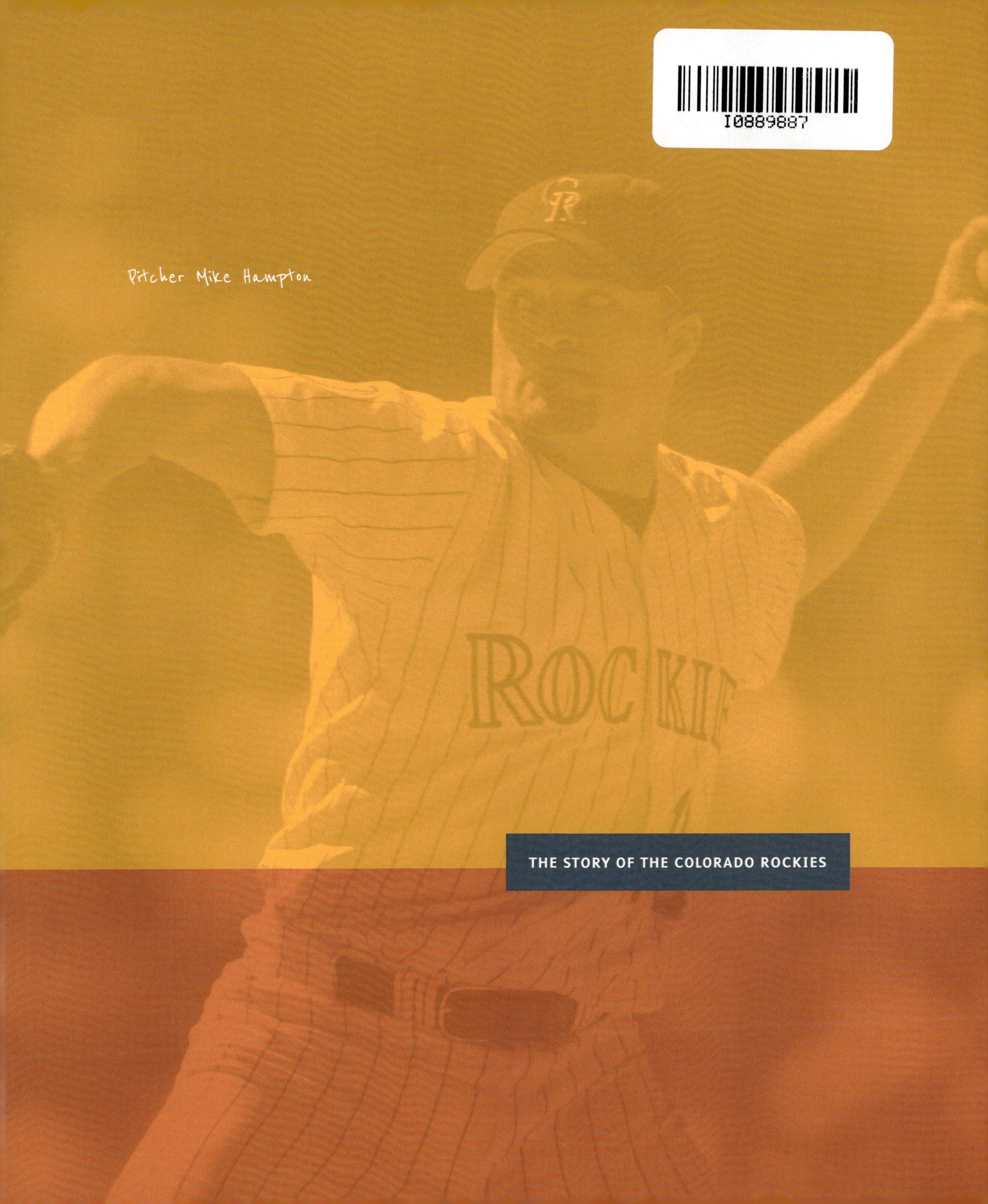

Pitcher Mike Hampton

THE STORY OF THE COLORADO ROCKIES

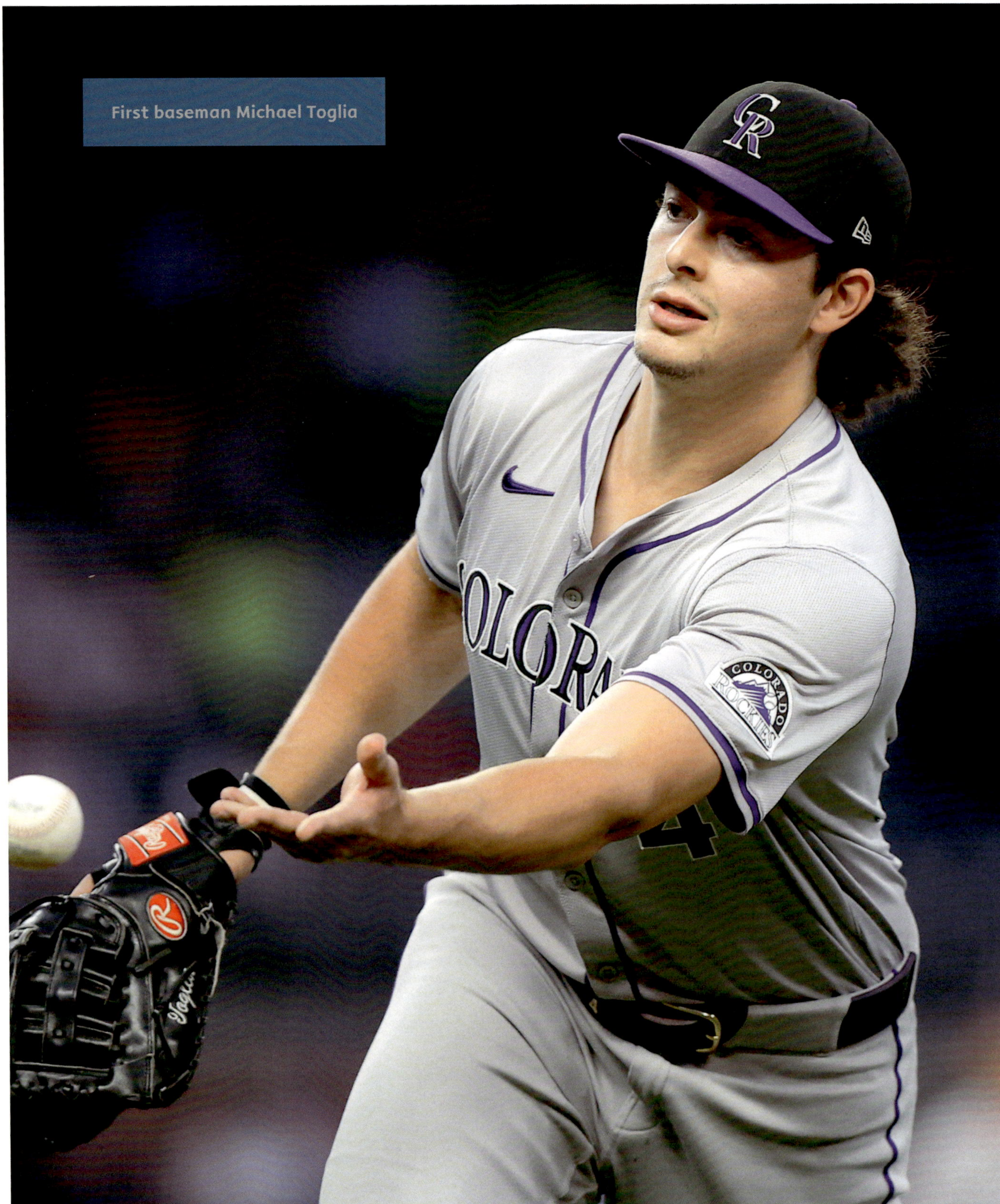

First baseman Michael Toglia

THE STORY OF THE

COLORADO ROCKIES

JIM WHITING

CREATIVE SPORTS

Second baseman Eric Young

CREATIVE EDUCATION / CREATIVE PAPERBACKS

Published by Creative Education and Creative Paperbacks
P.O. Box 227, Mankato, Minnesota 56002
Creative Education and Creative Paperbacks are imprints of
The Creative Company
www.thecreativecompany.us

Book Design by Wyeth Morgan
Art direction by Blue Design (www.bluedes.com)

Images by Alamy Stock Photo/Cal Sport Media, 31, PAT BENIC, 26–27; Associated Press/Kevin Langley/Icon Sportswire, cover, Marcio Jose Sanchez, 6 (top, left); Getty Images/Al Bello, 7 (bottom, right), Brian Bahr, 1, 6 (bottom, left), 6 (bottom, right), 18, 7 (top, left), 7 (bottom, left), 14, 29, CHRIS WILKINS, cover, 7 (top, right), DOUG COLLIER, 3, Doug Pensinger, 15, 20, Glenn Asakawa, 9, Jamie Squire, 22–23, Jed Jacobsohn, 19, Karl Gehring, 11, Lisa Blumenfeld, 6 (top, right), 25, Nathan Bilow, 16, Rob Leiter, 10, 30, Scott Boehm, 4–5, 32, Stephen Dunn, 12, Todd Kirkland, 2; Wikimedia Commons/Dirk DBQ, 10
Every effort has been made to contact copyright holders for material reproduced in this book. Any omissions will be rectified in subsequent printings if notice is given to the publisher.

Library of Congress Cataloging-in-Publication Data
Names: Whiting, Jim, 1943- author
Title: The story of the Colorado Rockies / by Jim Whiting.
Description: Mankato, Minnesota : Creative Education and Creative Paperbacks, [2026] | Series: Creative sports. Major League baseball | Includes index. | Audience: Ages 8-12 | Audience: Grades 4-6 | Summary: "Discover the Colorado Rockies' thrilling journey from their rocky start to playoff triumphs, highlighting legendary players, unforgettable moments, and the Major League Baseball team's enduring resilience and determination. Written for middle-grade readers. Includes table of contents, sidebars, and index"— Provided by publisher.
Identifiers: LCCN 2025013118 (print) | LCCN 2025013119 (ebook) | ISBN 9798895810927 library binding | ISBN 9798896800453 paperback | ISBN 9798895812181 ebook
Subjects: LCSH: Colorado Rockies (Baseball team)—History—Juvenile literature | Baseball—Colorado—History—Juvenile literature
Classification: LCC GV875.C78 W55 2026 (print) | LCC GV875.C78 (ebook) | DDC 796.357/640978883—dc23/eng/20250526
LC record available at https://lccn.loc.gov/2025013118
LC ebook record available at https://lccn.loc.gov/2025013119

Printed in the United States

Pitcher Aaron Cook

COLORADO
38

COLORADO
ROCKIES

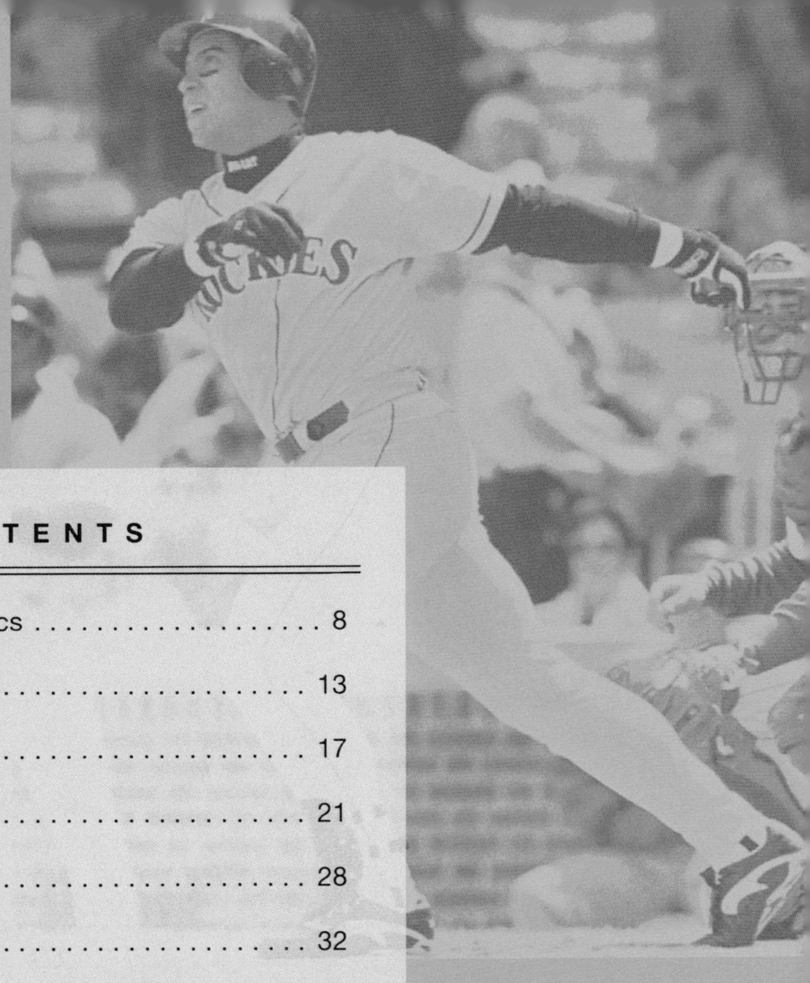

CONTENTS

EXTRA INNINGS

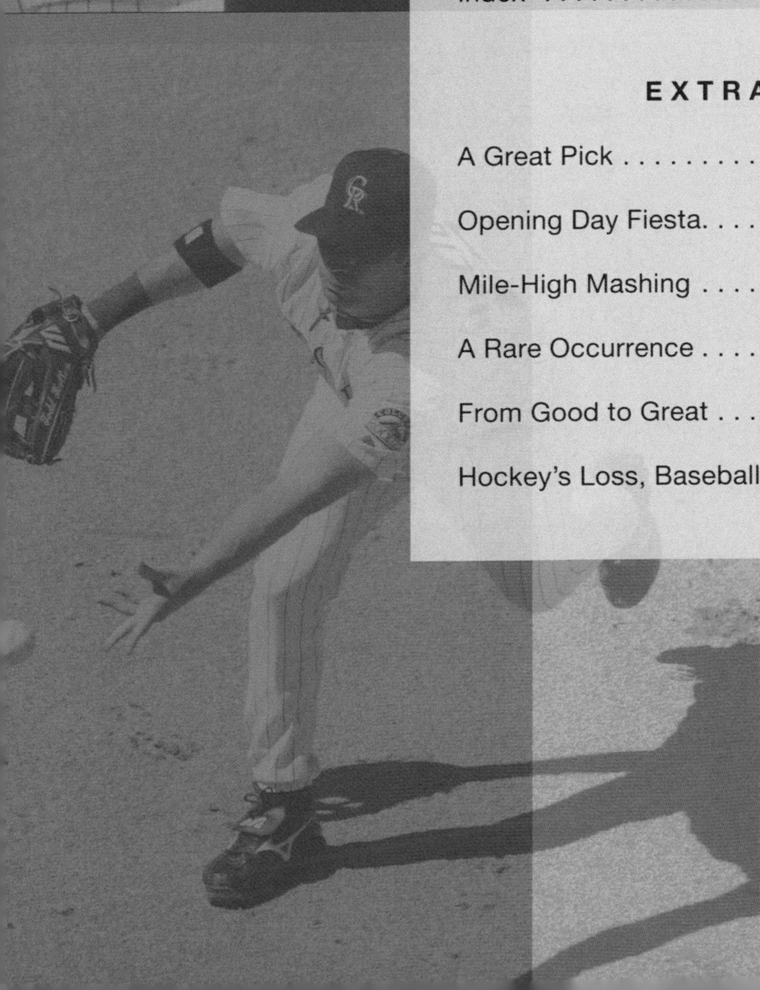

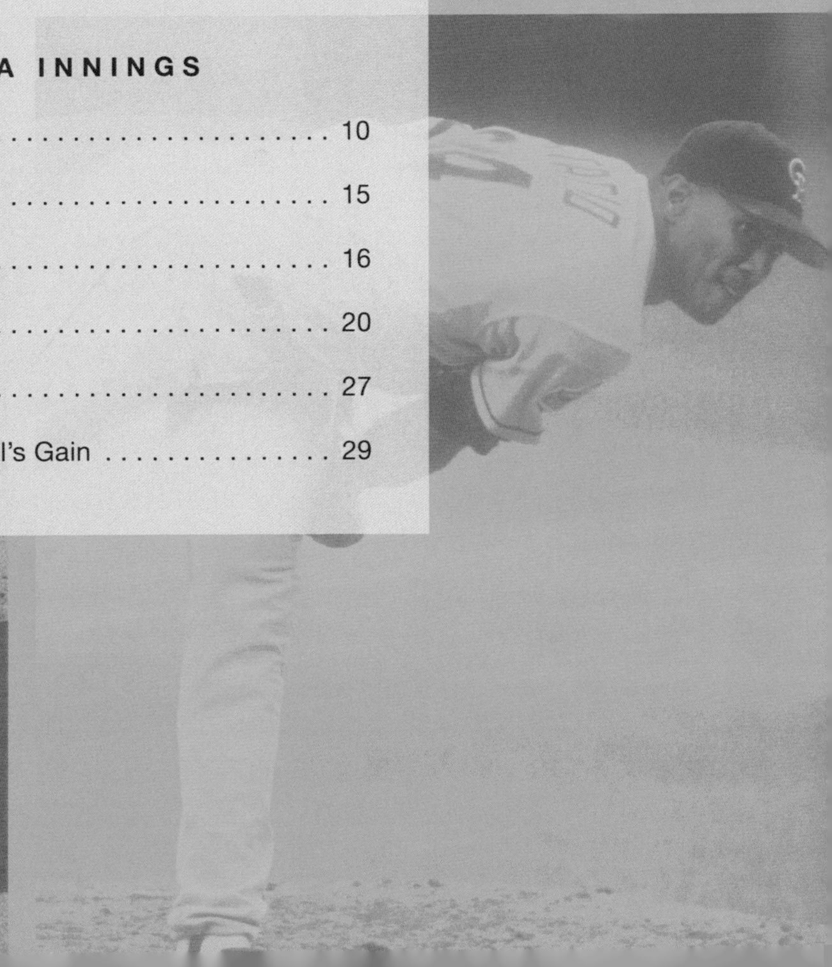

HOLLIDAY'S HEADFIRST HEROICS

In 2007, the Colorado Rockies' Major League Baseball (MLB) season got off to a rocky start. A loss to the Arizona Diamondbacks on May 21 dropped them to 18–27 (a .400 winning percentage). Then they caught fire. They went 71–46 (.607) for the rest of the season to finish 89–73. They won 13 of their last 14 games to tie with the San Diego Padres for the National League (NL) Wild Card Series.

The two teams met at Coors Field in Denver, Colorado, for a one-game playoff on October 1. The Rockies jumped out to a 3–0 lead after two innings. San Diego surged ahead in the next inning, 5–2. Colorado regained the lead in the sixth inning at 6–5, but the Padres knotted the score in the eighth inning at 6–6. The game went to extra innings.

A two-run homer in the top of the 13th gave San Diego an 8–6 lead. The Padres looked to Trevor Hoffman, one of the best closers in MLB, to close out the win. He was a six-time All-Star who had notched 42 saves during the regular season.

He wasn't up to the job. Rockies second baseman Kazuo Matsui led off the inning with a double. Shortstop Troy Tulowitzki followed with another double. Matsui scored. Left fielder Matt Holliday plated Tulowitzki with a triple off the right field

Left fielder Matt Holliday slides into home.

EXTRA INNINGS

TODD HELTON
FIRST BASEMAN
ROCKIES SEASONS: 1997–2013
HEIGHT: 6-FOOT-2
WEIGHT: 220 POUNDS
KEY STATS: .316 BATTING AVERAGE, 369 HOME RUNS, 1,406 RBIS, 2000 MLB LEADER IN RBIS WITH 147

A GREAT PICK

Todd Helton was named College Player of the Year in 1995. He was the Rockies' first choice and eighth overall in the 1997 MLB Amateur Draft. He made an immediate impact, finishing as runner-up in Rookie of the Year voting. He led the NL in batting in 2000 with a robust .372 mark, which also began a streak of five straight years as an All-Star. He nearly won a second batting title in 2003. An intentional walk in his final plate appearance resulted in an average of .35849, losing the title by .00022. Helton became one of a small number of players in the era of free agency who played their entire career with the same team. The team retired his jersey number (17) in 2014, a year after his final season. Helton was the first Rockies player with that honor. In 2024, he became just the second Colorado player elected to the Baseball Hall of Fame.

First baseman Todd Helton

Third baseman Jamey Carroll

wall. Hoffman intentionally walked first baseman Todd Helton, one of Colorado's best hitters. Third baseman Jamey Carroll came to the plate. He was a utility player who hit just .225 during the season. But he had a secret. "I knew that Hoffman usually tried to get ahead and get away with his fastball on the first pitch," he said. "So if there was ever a time to swing at a first pitch, that was it."

Carroll lifted Hoffman's first pitch into right field. Holliday tagged up and sprinted down the third-base line as Padres right fielder Brian Giles caught the ball and unleashed a hard throw to home plate. As the ball bounced in front of catcher Mike Barrett, Holliday dove headfirst with his left arm outstretched for the plate. Home plate umpire Tim McClellan hesitated briefly, then spread his arms and called "Safe!" as the ball skittered away from Barrett. The Rockies won 9–8! It was only the second time in the team's 15-year history that they advanced to the playoffs.

"It was a great game," said San Diego manager Bud Black, who later became the Colorado skipper. "Simply a tremendous game."

Franklin

MINING BASEBALL GOLD

Gold was discovered in Colorado in 1859. Prospectors and miners immediately poured into the state. The first recorded baseball game was played two years later. For many years as the state grew, fans wanted a major-league team. Their efforts finally paid off in the early 1990s. MLB awarded expansion NL franchises to Denver and Miami, Florida. The Denver team would play in the NL's West Division starting in 1993.

To emphasize the new team's statewide appeal, the owners kept "Colorado" in the name. They called their franchise the Rockies. "We feel very strongly that Colorado Rockies might be one of the strongest names in all of professional sports," said team CEO John Antonucci. "It's strong, enduring, majestic." The team's logo includes a purple mountain design. That alluded to the "purple mountain majesties" in the song "America the Beautiful."

Team officials started building the roster by choosing players from other franchises in an expansion draft. Draftees included third baseman Charlie Hayes, second baseman Eric Young, and catcher Joe Girardi. Another was outfielder Kevin Reimer. They immediately traded him to the Milwaukee Brewers for outfielder Dante Bichette. It was one of the team's best-ever trades. Reimer left the majors a year later. Bichette became a four-time All-Star. The Rockies also signed free agents. One was All-Star first baseman Andrés "Big Cat" Galarraga. He gave the lineup a legitimate hitter.

The Rockies played their first home game on April 9, 1993. More than 80,000 baseball-crazed fans packed Denver's Mile High Stadium. (The Rockies

Second baseman Eric Young

Coors Field, 1999

played two seasons there, sharing the space with the Denver Broncos of the National Football League while Coors Field was built.) Colorado faced the Montreal Expos. Young was the first Colorado batter in the game. He had a reputation for hitting singles. But that day, he stroked the 3–2 pitch into the left-field stands. The fans erupted. Colorado cruised to an 11–4 win. Interestingly, Young didn't hit another home run until the last home game of the season. The Rockies went on to compile a 67–95 record. They finished sixth in the NL West, six games ahead of San Diego. Galarraga hit .370. He was the NL batting champion.

Before the season, Rockies officials tried to predict the season attendance. Data suggested that 1.7 million was a reasonable figure. The data was wrong. The final tally was a whopping 4,483,350. At the time, that was more than the population of Colorado! It is still the MLB record. "Whether it was raining or snowing or whatever, it was a packed house every day," recalled third baseman Vinny Castilla.

MLB split into three divisions in 1994. Colorado was on its way to doing well in the newly formed four-team NL West Division. But a players' strike in mid-August brought the season to an abrupt end. The Rockies finished with a 53–64 mark.

THIRD BASEMAN VINNY CASTILLA

EXTRA INNINGS

OPENING DAY FIESTA

When people think of baseball, they think of hot dogs, Cracker Jacks, and ... burritos? The Rockies opened the 1999 season in Mexico. It was a special day for Vinny Castilla. The popular third baseman was from Mexico. In front of family, friends, and many admirers, Castilla went four for five. One hit was a double. He helped the Rockies crush the San Diego Padres 8–2. “I feel really excited I played in front of fans in my own country,” Castilla said. “I tried my last two at-bats to hit a home run. It didn’t happen, but I’m happy for the win.”

EXTRA INNINGS

MILE-HIGH MASHING

Coors Field is the ultimate hitter's park. Nearly a mile above sea level, the air there is thin. There is less air resistance on pitched balls. Breaking ball pitches such as curveballs and sliders need resistance to "break" away. Batted balls also travel faster and farther. There is also a unique challenge for Rockies players. "Going on the road after hitting in Colorado is hard," said first baseman Todd Helton. "The ball breaks more and it's a huge adjustment going the season, going through that rigorous grind and being able to make those changes midseason." In his career, Helton hit .345 with 227 home runs in 1,141 home games. He hit .287 with 142 long balls in 1,106 away games. The Rockies often lead the majors in runs scored at home.

MOUNTAIN MAGIC

The team made a splash in 1995. It signed power-hitting right fielder Larry Walker. He gave the team another long-ball threat. On April 26, the Rockies played their first game at Coors Field. They faced off against the New York Mets. The marathon game stretched 14 innings. Finally, Bichette launched a three-run homer. It gave Colorado an unforgettable 11–9 victory.

The Rockies finished the season 77–67. It placed them second in the NL West. They became only the second team in MLB history to have four players with at least 30 home runs apiece in a single season: Walker, Galarraga, Castilla, and Bichette. Together, the quartet slammed 139 home runs. That was more than 12 MLB teams' entire lineups! A local newspaper columnist dubbed them the "Blake Street Bombers." Coors Field was located on Denver's Blake Street.

Colorado's postseason hopes hinged on the final game of the season. Winning would earn a Wild Card berth. The Rockies pulled off a 10–9 comeback victory over the San Francisco Giants. "That was the coolest game I'd ever been a part of," said pitcher Curt Leskanic. The Rockies were in the playoffs in just their third season! They headed to the National League Division Series (NLDS) against the Atlanta Braves. Heavily favored to win, Atlanta beat the Rockies in four games.

The Rockies held steady at 83–79 the next two seasons. They missed the playoffs both years. But their offense was strong, especially at home. In 1996, Colorado became the first—and still the only—team to post 200 home runs and 200 stolen bases in the same season. Outfielders Ellis Burks and Bichette

First baseman Todd Helton

led the way. They became just the second pair of teammates with 30 home runs and 30 stolen bases apiece in the same season. Galarraga set a franchise record with a whopping 150 runs batted in (RBIs). The following year, Walker slugged his way to the NL's Most Valuable Player (MVP) award.

The team slumped to 77–85 in 1998. A season highlight occurred on June 10. Bichette became the first Rockies player to bat for the cycle: he hit a single, double, triple, and home run in the same game. A month and a half later, shortstop Neifi Pérez became the second. That same year, Helton was runner-up for Rookie of the Year. He hit .315. He smashed 25 homers and drove in 97 runs.

Despite such stellar individual performances, the Rockies struggled to find pitchers who could win consistently in the high altitude. Pedro Astacio tied a team record with 17 wins in 1999. He also struck out 210 batters. It remained a franchise record until 2010. But the team finished last in the NL West. It traded away fan favorites Castilla and Bichette.

Right fielder Larry Walker

EXTRA INNINGS

TROY TULOWITZKI
SHORTSTOP
ROCKIES SEASONS: 2006–14
HEIGHT: 6-FOOT-3
WEIGHT: 205 POUNDS
KEY STATS: .299 BATTING AVERAGE, 168 HOME RUNS, 657 RBIS, 5X ALL-STAR

A RARE OCCURRENCE

The Colorado Rockies hosted the Atlanta Braves on April 29, 2007. In the seventh inning, Atlanta's Kelly Johnson was on second. Edgar Rentería was on first. Chipper Jones smacked a line drive left of second base. Tulowitzki snagged the ball. One out. He dashed to second base and stepped on the bag. Two outs. Then he tagged Rentería, who was running to second base. Three outs. It was an unassisted triple play! Only 12 players had done that before Tulowitzki. Since then, two more players have executed unassisted triple plays. It remains one of the rarest—and most memorable—feats in major-league ball.

Colorado's 2000 roster featured several new players known more as high-average hitters than long-ball sluggers. These included third baseman Jeff Cirillo and right fielder Jeffrey Hammonds. The team also added speedy rookie Juan Pierre in center field. But pitching problems continued to haunt the Rockies. They finished the season at 82–80 and out of the playoffs.

REACHING NEW HEIGHTS

Before the 2001 season, the Rockies signed Denny Neagle and Mike Hampton. They were the top two free-agent pitchers. Both jumped off to quick starts. But the thin mountain air eventually took its toll. Both left the team within three years. It was an expensive failed experiment.

The Rockies believed they had found their elusive pitching star in Jason Jennings. In 2001, Jennings became the first man in MLB history to pitch a shutout and hit a home run in his debut. Jennings went 16–8 the next year. But he could not match that success in the following seasons. He left, too.

Colorado was scoring lots of runs. But they were giving up even more. The team remained stuck near the bottom of the NL West standings through 2006.

Tulowitzki's 2007 callup to the big leagues turned out to be just what the team needed. In May, Colorado fell nine games under .500. The brash rookie screamed at his teammates, "This team is too good to be playing like this!"

Left fielder Matt Holliday

HOLLIDAY
5

Tulowitzki was right. His outburst seemed to wake up the team. They tied the Padres in the season's final game and won the memorable tiebreaker. It was the team's first postseason appearance in 12 years. "We turned a corner as a franchise," said general manager Dan O'Dowd, "and the biggest reason for that was Troy .... He's one of those very rare players who makes players around him better."

The Rockies swept the Philadelphia Phillies in the NLDS in three games. They knocked off the Arizona Diamondbacks in four straight games in the National League Championship Series (NLCS). That gave the Rockies their first-ever NL pennant. The team had won 21 games of their last 22 in the regular season and playoffs. The Rockies faced the powerful Boston Red Sox in the World Series.

Unfortunately, Colorado's magic faded. The Red Sox crushed the Rockies in Game 1, 13–1. Colorado took a quick 1–0 lead in Game 2. Holliday had four hits. But his teammates had only one hit among them. Boston eked out a 2–1 win. Then the Red Sox banged out 15 hits for 10 runs in Game 3 and won easily. A late Colorado rally in Game 4 fell just short. Boston held on for a 4–3 win and the world title.

The Rockies suffered through a subpar 2008 season with a 74–88 record. The following year, they were stuck in last place in the division by early June. Then they caught fire. They surged to a franchise-record 92 wins. It was an 18-game improvement over 2008. Jim Tracy was named Manager of the Year. The Rockies earned a Wild Card entry. But the Phillies beat them in four games in the NLDS.

In 2010, Tulowitzki and young outfielder Carlos González provided steady slugging. Pitcher Ubaldo Jiménez won 19 games. That set a new team record. The Rockies stayed in the hunt for the division title most of the season. Then a late cold streak dropped their record to 83–79. They missed the playoffs.

Pitcher Ubaldo Jiménez

COLORADO
38

NOLAN ARENADO
THIRD BASE
ROCKIES SEASONS: 2013–20
HEIGHT: 6-FOOT-2
WEIGHT: 215 POUNDS
KEY STATS: .293 BATTING AVERAGE, 341 HOME RUNS, 1,132 RBIS, 5X ALL-STAR

EXTRA INNINGS

FROM GOOD TO GREAT

When the Rockies drafted Nolan Arenado in the second round of the 2013 MLB Draft, they knew he was an excellent hitter. His defense, not so much. “I had really bad feet,” he said. “I was too lazy.” His minor league manager, Jerry Weinstein, worked with him to improve his play in the field. The hard work paid off. He won eight Gold Glove awards, four Silver Slugger awards, and was a five-time All-Star with the Rockies. “In an era ripe with great third basemen, Arenado is arguably the best,” said Jeff Passan of Yahoo Sports. Fans were dismayed when the team traded Arenado to St. Louis for five prospects after the 2020 season. Only two of those prospects played for the Rockies, and neither had much of an impact.

PEAKS AND VALLEYS

Unfortunately, 2010 was the team's last winning season for several years. Helton retired in 2013 as a five-time All-Star. He won the Silver Slugger award four times and the Gold Glove award three times. In the same year, fans had a new player to cheer for. Rookie third baseman Nolan Arenado won the Gold Glove award and hit .301.

The Rockies finished 75–87 in 2016. They flipped that mark the following year and made it into the Wild Card game. They faced the Diamondbacks. Arizona held on for an 11–8 win.

Colorado did even better in 2018. It won 91 games. It tied with the Los Angeles Dodgers for the NL West Division title. The Dodgers won a one-game playoff. But Colorado still qualified for the postseason. It was the first time in team history with back-to-back playoff appearances. The Rockies faced the Chicago Cubs in the Wild Card game. With the score tied 1–1 in top of the 13th inning, catcher Tony Wolters's two-out single scored shortstop Trevor Story to give Colorado the lead. Relief pitcher Scott Oberg struck out the side in the bottom of the inning to clinch the 2–1 victory. But the Brewers swept them in the NLDS as the Rockies managed just two runs in the three-game series.

The team had high hopes for the 2019 season. It was in Wild Card position by late June, but the Rockies crumbled in the rest of the season. The team's 71–91 record was one of the worst in the NL.

Before the 2020 season, Larry Walker became the first Colorado player voted into the Baseball Hall of Fame! But his induction wouldn't happen for more than a year. The Covid-19 pandemic led to a shortened season. The Rockies compiled a 26–34 record.

EXTRA INNINGS

LARRY WALKER
OUTFIELD/FIRST BASE
ROCKIES SEASONS: 1995–2004
HEIGHT: 6-FOOT-2
WEIGHT: 185 POUNDS
KEY STATS: .334 BATTING AVERAGE, 258 HOME RUNS, 848 RBIS, 4X ALL-STAR

HOCKEY'S LOSS, BASEBALL'S GAIN

Growing up in British Columbia, Canada, Larry Walker dreamed of glory as a goalkeeper in professional hockey. But he was just a third-stringer on his junior team before being cut. "It's a game I miss," Walker said. "I grew up playing it." He switched his athletic ambitions to baseball and signed with the Montreal Expos. In six years with the Expos, he hit .281 and won two Gold Gloves. He was even better when he joined Colorado. He became the first player since Al Simmons of the Philadelphia Athletics (1929–31) to hit above .360 in three straight seasons (1997–99). "He's the most talented player I've ever had," said manager Don Baylor. "All you have to do is write his name down in the lineup and he'll take care of the rest."

Outfielder Charlie Blackmon

Baseball returned to a full schedule in 2021. Colorado finished 74–87. Things continued to get worse. The Rockies went 68–94 in 2022. Then they finished 59–105 in 2023, the worst season in team history. The low point came on Saturday, June 24. The Rockies suffered a 25–1 smackdown from the Los Angeles Angels. Ironically, Colorado took the games on Friday and Sunday to win the three-game series.

The Rockies were almost as bad in 2024, winning just 61 games. It was their sixth straight losing season. One of the few highlights came in July. Helton was inducted into the Hall of Fame. "Competing on the baseball field was where I felt like I belonged," he said. "I liked putting in the long hours and doing the extra work."

For more than 25 years, baseball fans in the mountainous West have faithfully followed the Rockies. They have been treated to one of the most consistently powerful offenses in baseball. To them, there is no more fitting place for the "Mile-High City" than atop the baseball world. They eagerly anticipate the day when the Rockies will hoist the World Series trophy for the first time.

Shortstop Ezequiel Tovar

INDEX